ARE WE THERE YET?
Gone

ARE WE THERE YET?
Gone

BILLY SANDERS

authorHOUSE®

AuthorHouse™
1663 Liberty Drive
Bloomington, IN 47403
www.authorhouse.com
Phone: 1-800-839-8640

Published by AuthorHouse 10/02/2014

ISBN: 978-1-4969-4437-5 (sc)
ISBN: 978-1-4969-4439-9 (e)

Contents

Introduction

Sometime ago God laid it on my heart to write a book relating to the second coming of Christ, this is not to be an in-depth study of prophecy, but a kind of running account of where we are today.

All scripture in this book will be in the King James Version, unless noted.

I have entitled this book "ARE WE THERE YET?" This is in honor of all children who have had to endure a long tiring trip, and to all parents who have had to answer there question, by saying, "just a little further." My wife would usually add these words, sit back and be quiet, "we will be there soon." So I want to say to you children, sit back and enjoy the ride, but stay busy for the Lord, for we will be there soon. I am speaking of Christ coming in the air for his church, and the second coming to establish his kingdom here on the earth. After I had chosen the title above, I then thought of another title, "GONE!" I then decided to use the two titles together. This is not a time to go up on a mountain top to watch for His descent in the air to receive us. While the words of Jesus tells us that man cannot know the day or the hour of his return, but we are to know and interpret the signs of the times. Jesus proclaimed a wicked and adulterous generation for being unable to interpret the signs of the times, in his days.

Billy Sanders

"He answered and said unto them,
When it is evening, ye say, it will

Be fair weather: for the sky is red. And in the morning,
it will be foul weather today: for the sky is red and
lowring. O ye hypocrites, ye can discern the face of the
sky: But can ye not discern the signs of the times?
(Matthew 16:3)

But what about this day in which we live, as a songwriter wrote, "The signs of the times are everywhere." In this book, I will lay out some things that have already happened. Israel had to be restored as a nation, and this happened in 1948, I see this time as the countdown to the end and of things as we know them.

Chapter I

Are We There Yet

"All Scripture is given by inspiration
of God, and is profitable

For doctrine, for reproof, for correction in righteousness."
11 Tim. 3: 16

The answer to the question, Are We There Yet? Is no. If we were there, there would not be one born again Christian left upon this earth. They would be GONE! But soon, very soon! The rapture of the church is described in First Thessalonians,

> *"For this we say unto you by the word of the Lord,*
> *that we which are alive and remain unto the coming*
> *of the Lord shall not prevent them which are asleep.*
> *For the Lord himself shall descend from heaven with*
> *a shout, with the voice of the archangel, and with the*
> *trump of God; and the dead in Christ shall rise first;*
> *Then we which are alive and remain shall be caught*

> *up together with them in the clouds, to meet the Lord*
> *in the air; and so shall we ever be with the Lord.*
> *(1 Thessalonians 4:15-17)*

In the book of Revelation, chapter one concerning Jesus Christ. There is a vision of the resurrected and risen Savior and near the end of chapter one Jesus declares that he is alive for evermore. Chapter 2 and 3 consist of the messages Our Lord sent to the seven churches, of course there was and is many more churches than these seven churches, but these represent the seven Church ages. Seven is the number for completion. The seventh and last church to be mentioned is the church of the Laodicea's.

> *"And unto the angel of the church of the of the*
> *Laodiceans write; These things saith the Amen, the*
> *faithful and true witness, the beginning of the creation*
> *of God; I know thy works that thou art neither cold*
> *or hot; I would thou wert cold or hot. So then because*
> *thou art lukewarm and nether cold nor hot, I will*
> *spew the out of my mouth."… (Rev. 3:14-16)*

> *"To him that overcometh will I grant to set with*
> *me in my throne, even as I also overcame, and*
> *am set down with my Father in His throne."*
> *(Rev. 3:21)*

That is the age that the church is in today, and I believe we are at the very end of this church age. What happens when God declares that the age of the church is over? The answer to that question is pictured in chapter four of the book of Revelation.

"After this I looked and behold a door was opened in heaven; and the first voice which I heard was as it were of a trumpet talking with me: which said, Come up hither, and I will shew thee things which must be here after." (Rev. 4:1)

Very soon that door will be opened, and we who have been born again, will hear a voice calling us to come up here, the church will be GONE! All that is described in the book of Revelation after chapter three, are events that take place after the church raptures up into heaven. Of course there is the dark side of what our Lord is trying to reveal unto to us. Satan does not want you to know, what is about to happen in these last days. But Satan is a liar and a deceiver. "Thus smith the Lord!" Our Savior He is the final answer to every lie of Satan. Evil men and deceivers are going to get worse and worse, they will deceive more and more. Why? Because they are being deceived by Satan! In these last days, there will be more word deception; and the only way a believer will be able to tell the truth from the false is by knowing the word of God. The only way to defeat Satan's lies is with the word of God's truth.

****

To every believer in the Lord Jesus Christ: This is a **Special Message** to you. There is one thing that our Lord Jesus expects from every child of His, and that is to be a witness for him. Also as you will understand as we move forward, that you are to recognize the times that we are in. And through your love, your compassion, and concern, for your love ones, and your friends, that you will do everything in your power to introduce them to Jesus! Remember that you will receive rewards when you stand before the Lord. Don't be ashamed but rejoice in the Lord.

****

Notes and Reflections:

Notes and Reflections:

Notes and Reflections:

Chapter II

A little while back I put out notes on regular bases that I entitled, "Billy's Notes." I sent these out to friends and family, and to a few churches. In order to illustrate, "that the signs of the times are everywhere." I will rerun some of them, in part now. Jesus condemned the Pharisees and Sadducees because they would not believe' and therefore they could not believe. Would the above be a fair statement concerning some church leaders today? One of the causes of unbelief is stated in the following scripture.

> *"But though he had done so many miracles before them, yet they believed not on him; That the saying of Esaias the prophet might be fulfilled, which he spoke, Lord who hath believed our report? And to whom hath the arm of the Lord been revealed?*
> *(John12:37-38)*

> *"And that, knowing the time, that now it is high time to awake out of sleep: for now is our salvation nearer than we believed."*
> *(Romans 13:11.)*

Our salvation nearer then when we believed" DR. JP Mac Beth's comment on the above, in part says, "… this incentive is that we are about to step into eternal glories. We are nearer heaven, than when we believed, and we ought to journey in the light of our home. We ought to live with reference to our eternal salvation. The rapid approach of our consummated salvation ought to heighten the moral character of our citizenship."

> *"Not forsaking the assembling of ourselves together, as the*
> *matter of some is; but exhorting one another; and so much*
> *the more as you see the day approaching" (Heb. 10:25)*

Dr. Wiersby says "absenting themselves from the church fellowship. It is interesting to note that the emphasis here is not on what a believer gets from the assembly, but rather on what he can contribute to the assembly. Faithfulness in church attendance encourages others and provokes them to love and good works." My note here is to church leaders. HELP! No, not for me (even though I am sure my pastor would agree, I need help,) but rather help your people to see" the day is approaching." And thereby help them to be more faithful to the Lord Jesus and his church, and help them to be more loving, caring, forgiving, and giving, of self and resources. Remember the notes, that I will share from my files are events that have already passed, and will only include a news article, and a short passage of Scripture, the entire note of each week will not be complete. I will assign a number to each article, and probably not in order as they happened.

Number one:

In the news; "a 14-year-old boy, shot his father, mother, and grandmother, this is one of many such reports in recent times.

Number two

Bill Ayers; 1960 "Kill your parents."

(Jesus)

> *"Do you suppose that I came to grant peace on*
> *earth? I tell you no, but rather division; for from now*
> *on five members in one household will be divided,*
> *three against two, and two against three. Father*
> *against son and son against father, mother against*
> *daughter and daughter against her mother, mother-*
> *in law against daughter- in law and daughter-in law*
> *against mother-in law. (Luke. 12: 51-56.)NKJ*

Why do you not analyze this present time?

Number three:

Recently; China's President had just landed, and it was reported. They wanted to propose a post American global ration, that it is time to stop using the dollar as the world's monetary standard. On many fronts there is a move to bring down our Western way of life, and to destroy our economy, some of them are right here in this country.

> *"And that no one may buy or sell except one who*
> *has the mark or the name of the beast, or the*
> *number of his name." (Rev. 13:17, NKJ).*

Number four:

Bill Ayers, in the Middle East teaching how a New World order could be brought in.

Number five:

George Soros, "Israel and the USA are the main problem to a just order."

Number six:

The British, France, Germany, has shown that "multi-cultures has failed, Glen Beck reports from a number of sources such as, Muslim brotherhood, code pink, Marxism, that a new world order is coming. The European Union will be the catalyst for one of the new World orders, and attempt to be the only one.

Notes and Reflections:

Notes and Reflections:

Notes and Reflections:

Chapter III

"Are We There Yet?"

The signs of the times are everywhere; THINGS THAT ARE YET TO HAPPEN: Types and shadows of some of these things may happen before I finish writing this book. But the real tribulation will be after God takes his church out of this world; and will be much worse than the types and shadows; we are speaking of the time known as the rapture. But as we look at the event's that has recently taken place, we can see that this time is drawing nearer, up heaves in nature, signs in the sky, murders greatly on the increase, robbery, sexually immorality, corruption in government. Yes we have always had these things, but not to the extent they are happening today, nor nearly as bad today as they will be after the influence of the church is removed from the this world.

Things are happening so fast today that point to the impending rapture of the church that before I can finish this book, I have to go back and insert more up to date news articles.

In the news: John Ledue planned to kill his mother, and sister, and then he planned to blow up his high school. I believe this speaks of the increase of demon possession in the world today, and of the growing immorality. Someone reported his suspicious moves and he was arrested before he could carry out his devilish plan.

Somewhere between two hundred, and three hundred girls kidnapped maybe more, in South Africa. These were from the Christian section of Africa, and they threaten to sell them across the border as wives (sex slaves).

On the local news, it is reported that there is seventy five million people drunk, and it is expected to grow to another ten million.

Drones; not only is this part of the fulfillment of the last chapter of Daniel, There is the potential to kill people, and that has already been demonstrated, they will be able to tract people, now and especially during the tribulation, spy on people, and I believe that privacy may soon be a thing of the past, it probably is now more than most people think.

CYBER Space: Just today, 5\13\14, it was announced on TV that there are companies that are gathering your private information, and selling this information to other companies, and making millions on these sells.

Jeremiah Chapter six speaks of the destruction of Jerusalem that is impending; it also calls attention to the gentile's nations in several verses. The things of this chapter have been going on for some time, and reaches beyond today into the seven years of tribulation. The judgment that is true of the Israelites is also true of the gentiles that have not believed in the Lord.

My four daughters are all grown up now and have families of their own, but in there dating years there was a discussion about advertising feminine products over T.V. It was not that young ladies didn't need them. But that greedy merchant wanted them to use their brand. I was very upset because much of the dating of our daughters was dating on the couch in our living room, and I knew they would be embarrassed in front of their boyfriends. And the boys would also be embarrassed. Well, today we have moved far beyond that and that is not a good thing. Jeremiah writing the words of God for us wrote:

"Were they ashamed when they had committed an
abomination? Nay, they were not at all ashamed,
neither could they <u>blush:</u> therefore they shall fall among
them that fall: at the time that I visit them they shall
be cast down, saith the Lord. (Jeremiah 6:15)

(Neither could they blush!) With all they show on TV today I believe this is an accurate statement for this day and time. ARE WE THERE YET? But God always holds out hope for any who will listen.

****

To everyone who has not yet trusted in the Lord Jesus Christ; this is a Special Message to you: Hundred's and hundred's of prophecies from the beginning of time, that were suppose to be fulfilled up until this time, has been, and all further prophecies will be fulfilled. Jesus himself said,

"For verily I say un to you, till heaven and earth
pass, one jot or one tittle shall in no wise pass from
the law, till all be fulfilled. (Matthew 5:18)

The signs of the time indicate that soon, very soon! The church will be gone! And only those who have not received Jesus will be left to go through the tribulation. WHY WOULD YOU DO THAT? You can't be good enough, can't work yourself to heaven, but what you can do is tell Jesus the Savior, "Jesus right now I trust you as my Lord and my Savior, and I ask your forgiveness for my sins.

****

Before moving on I need to tell you of some wars that are passed since 1948, and is yet future, these events are described in part in Psalms 83. As you read this psalm, you will find the old world names, and they may not make a lot of sense to you. These are the nations that have fought against Israel since 1948, and these are the nations that most nearly surround Israel. In order to identify these nations, one must compare the maps that go back much further in history with modern day maps. You would find that the modern names would include Jordan, Egypt, Arabia, Iraq, Lebanon, Syria, part of Turkey. All of these are people who would like to see Israel completely destroyed, and never to be a nation again. There is one country that you would expect to be in the list of nations above, that is the nation of Iran, (Persia) though they have given supported to the other nations yet, they have not been directly involved, even though they have the same goals and hatred for the nation of Israel. We will see just a little bit later that they will be involved; this will be brought out later. Psalms 83 is a prayer for Israel's defense. It is also prophecy.

They have said, Come, and let us cut them off from being
a nation; that the name of Israel may be no more in

remembrance. For they have consulted together with one consent; they are confederate against thee; The tabernacle of Edom, and the Ishmaelites; of Moab, and Hagerenes; Gebal, and Ammon, and Amelak; the Philistines with the inhabitants of Tyre; Assur also is joined with them; they have holpen the children of Lot. Selah. (Psalms 83:4-8)

There are some thing's that the Bible teaches us that is yet to happen, they are events that will take place after the rapture. I am sure that they will take place, but I am not sure of the chronological order in which they are to happen. I know that Israel will become one nation, that Israel and Judah will again be one nation, as in the beginning,

Then He said to me, "Son of man, these bones is the whole house of Israel; behold they say, 'Our bones are dried up and our hope is perished. We are completely cut off.' Therefore prophesy, and say to them, thus says the Lord God, "Behold, I will open your graves and cause you to come up out of your graves, my people; and I will bring you into the land of Israel. (graves refer to the lands that they had been dispersed to) …" and I will put My Spirit within you, and you will come to life, and I will place you in your own land. Then you will know that I, the Lord have spoken and done it," declares the Lord."' The word of the Lord came again to me saying, "And you son of man, take for yourself one stick and write on it, for Judah and for the sons of Israel, his companions'; then take another stick and write on it, 'For Joseph, the stick of Ephraim and for all the house of Israel, his companions.' Then Join them for yourself one to another in to one sticks that they may become one in your hand. … Say to them, thus says the Lord God," behold I will take the sons of Israel from

among the nations which they have gone, and I will gather
them from every side and bring them into their own land;
(Ezekiel 37:11-21.)

I also know that Israel will possess all the land that God gave them back in the Old Testament. They have not yet possessed all the land that God gave them. But they will! Also, God will bring all of the Israelites back home.

"Let the redeemed of the Lord say so' whom He
has redeemed from the hand of the adversary. And
gathered from the lands, from the east and from
the west, from the north and from the south."
(Psalm. 107: 2-3 NASB).

Then it will come about in that day that the nations
will resort to the root of Jesse. Who will stand
as a signal for the peoples; and His resting place
will be glorious. (Isaiah 11: 10-12, NASB).

"And say to them. "Thus says the Lord God, Behold.
I will take the sons of Israel from among the nations
where they have gone, and I will gather them from
every side and bring them into there own land.
(Ezek. 37: 21, NASB).

There will not be one Jew left in America, or Russia or any part of the earth except the land that God has given them. But there will be much suffering and trials before then. Chapter 36 of the book of Ezekiel describes blessings on Israel.

God describes in verse seven of this chapter, that those nations that are around Israel will bear their own shame.

Therefore thus saith the Lord God; I have lifted
up my mine hand, surely the heathen that are
about you, they shell bear their shame.
(Ezekiel 36:7)

In verse 15 of this chapter, God promises a time that Israel will not hear the taunts of other nations anymore,

"Nor will I let you hear the taunts of the nations
anymore, nor bear the reproach of the peoples anymore,
nor shall you cause your nation to stumble anymore,"
says the Lord God.' "(Ezekiel 36: 15, NKJ)

Then chapter 36 continues on to describe the renewal of Israel. As we write God is moving quickly towards the finish line. Today, August 27, 2013, our president with other leaders is trying to figure out what to do about Syria, who has been accused of killing their own people with chemical weapons.

Here is something I know is going to happen, though I do not know just when it will happen. First, I know that Damascus will be destroyed, the capitol of Syria, and Syria itself will be taken over by Israel.

"Damascus is waxed feeble and turneth, herself to flee,
and fear has seized on her; anguish and sorrows have
taken her, as a woman in travail. How is the city of
praise not left, the city of my joy! Therefore her young
men shall fall in her streets, and all the men of war shall
be cut off in that day, saith the Lord of hosts. And I
will kindle a fire in the wall of Damascus, and it shall
consume the palaces of Ben-hadad." (Jeremiah 49:24-27)

*"The Burden of Damascus, Behold Damascus is taken
away from being a city, and it shall be a ruinous heap.
The cities of Aroer are forsaken: they shall be for
flocks, which shall lie down, and none shall make them
afraid. The fortress also shall cease from Ephraim,
and the kingdom from Damascus, and the remnant
of Syria: They shall be as the glory of the children
of Israel, saith the Lord of host." (Isaiah 17:1-3)*

I also know that God has laid out the borders of the nation of Israel, these can be found in (Numbers 34:2.) Though some of the names found in Numbers, are even older than those found in Psalms 83, yet when tracing the two of these on a map the borders of Israel will come out the same. Not only does God know, every Israelite, and when he will bring them all home. He even knows which tribe that each one belongs to. And he has allotted each tribe there portion as it will be in the kingdom age. The division of the land is well described in Chapter 48 of Ezekiel. To really understand what Israel will be like in the kingdom age, with the sanctuary in the center of its land and Jerusalem that will serve as the capital of the world. One needs to read this chapter of Ezekiel. God is going to bring judgment on those nations that have been warring with Israel since 1948,

*"Therefore thus the Lord God; I have lifted
up my hand, surely the heathen that are
about you, they shall bear their shame."
(Ezekiel 36:7.)*

The Lord is going to bring judgment on all the world during the tribulation, but in the above Scripture He is speaking of those around Israel. Also, God will pour out blessings on his people, Israel.

*"But ye, O mountains of Israel, ye shall shoot forth your
branches, and yield your fruit to my people of Israel; for
they are at hand to come. For behold I am for you, and I
will turn unto you, and ye shall be tilled and sown; And
I will multiply men upon you, all the house of Israel, even
all of it; and the cities shall be inhabited, and the wastes
shall be builded; And I will multiply upon you men and
beast; and they shall increase and bring fruit; and I will
settle you after your old estates, and will do better unto you
than at your beginnings; and ye shall know that I am the
Lord." Yea I will cause men to walk upon you, even my
people Israel; and they shall possess thee, and thou shalt
be their inheritance, and thou shalt no more henceforth
bereave them of men. Thus saith the Lord God; Because
they say unto you, Thou land devourest up men, and hast
bereaved thy nations; therefore thou shalt devour men
no more, neither bereave thy nations anymore, saith the
Lord God. Neither will I cause men to hear in thee the
shame of the heathen anymore, neither shalt thou bear
the reproach of the people any more, neither shalt thou
cause thy nations to fall anymore, saith the Lord God.*
(Ezekiel 36:8-15.)

Then in verses 23 to 28 this passage describes God's people having
an experience much like we have, when we are born aging, only this will
be on a massive scale, all of that nation will be saved at once.

*"Therefore say unto the house of Israel, thus saith the
Lord God; I do not this for your sakes, o house of
Israel, but for my holy name's sake, which you profaned
in the mist of them; and the heathen shall know that*

> *I am the Lord, saith the Lord God, When I shall be*
> *sanctified in you before their eyes. (Ezekiel 36:22-23)*

In Ezekiel Chapter 37, describes this same event, but in a different manner. This is about the "Valley of dry bones." I will try to interpret some of the words for those who might need them. Number one, the dry bones represent the lost Israelites, verse 6, 7, and 8, describes them back in their land standing on their feet, but they are spiritually dead. And in verse nine, they are to be breathed upon by the four winds. (In the Hebrew wind, and spirit, are the same word.) This is God's Spirit breathed into them which makes them a live; they already had physical life, now they will have spiritual and eternal life.

> *Thus saith the Lord God unto these bones; Behold, I will*
> *cause breath to enter into you, and ye shall live: And I will*
> *lay sinews upon you, and will bring up flesh upon you, and*
> *cover you with skin, and put breath in you, and ye shall live;*
> *and ye shall know that I am the Lord. So I prophesied as I*
> *was commanded; and as I prophesied, there was a noise, a*
> *shaking, bone to his bone. And when I beheld, lo, the sinews*
> *and the flesh came upon them, and the skin covered them*
> *above; but there were no breath in them. Then said he unto*
> *me, prophesy unto the wind, prophesy, son of man, and say*
> *to the wind, thus saith the Lord God; Come from the four*
> *wind, O breath and breath upon these slain, that they may*
> *live. (Ezekiel 37:5-9)*

Notes and Reflections:

Notes and Reflections:

Notes and Reflections:

Chapter IV

Daniel Chapter Two

ARE WE THERE YET; "The signs of the times are everywhere." Most prophecy relates to the Hebrew people, there land, and their Messiah.

The Babylon King, Nebuchadnezzar had conquered Jerusalem and taken many of their brightest young men to serve in his court. In Daniel two, the King had a dream that greatly disturbed him. After calling for his court, he then commanded that if they could not tell him what he had dreamed and what the dream meant that all of them would be put to death, this included Daniel and his friends. Then Daniel persuaded the king's guard to buy him and his like minded friend's time to pray. Then God appeared to Daniel in a night vision and revealed to him what the king's dream was, and also what it meant. Daniel then blessed, praised, and exalted the God of heaven (vv 19-23). Then Daniel was brought before the king, who asks him if he was able to make known to him the dream, which I have seen, and its interpretation? Daniel seized the opportunity to witness for the God of heaven. Then Daniel said, "There is a God in heaven who reveals to King Nebuchadnezzar what will be in the latter days." We now come to the dream itself. Jesus speaks of this time, as from the crucifixion to the fall of Jerusalem. "And they will fall by the edge of the sword, and be led away captive into all nations.

> *"And Jerusalem will be trampled by the Gentiles*
> *until the times of the Gentiles are fulfilled."*

The dream and its interpretation;

> *Thou, O king, sawest, and behold a great image, this great*
> *image, whose brightness was excellent, stood before thee;*
> *and the form thereof was terrible. This image's head was*
> *of fine gold, his breast and his arms of silver, his belly and*
> *his thighs of brass. His legs of iron, his feet part of iron*
> *and part of clay. Thou sawest till that a stone was cut out*
> *without hands, which smote the image upon his feet that*
> *were of iron and clay, and brake them to pieces. Then was*
> *the iron, and clay, the brass, the silver, and the gold, broken*
> *to pieces together, and became like the chaff of the summer*
> *threshing floor; and the wind carried them away, that no*
> *place was found for them; and the stone that smote the*
> *image became a great mountain, and filled the whole earth.*
> *(Daniel 2:31-35)*

How will it all turn out, I will skip a few verses, and go to verses 44, and 45 to demonstrate how this will all end.

> *And in the days of these kings shall the God of heaven*
> *set up a kingdom, which shall never be destroyed; and*
> *the kingdom shall not be left to other people, but it shall*
> *break in pieces and consume all these kingdoms, and it*
> *shall stand for ever. Forasmuch as thou sawest that the*
> *stone was cut out of the mountain with out hands, and*
> *that it brake in pieces the iron, the brass, the clay, the*
> *silver, and the gold; the great God hath made known*

> *to the king <u>what shall come to pass hereafter</u>; and the*
> *dream is certain, and the interpretation thereof sure.*
> *(Daniel 2: 44-45)*

In chapter two, and three of the book of Revelation, Jesus has spoken of the church age that ends with the last verse of chapter three. Chapter four verses one begins with what will happen when the church is gone. Even though I had already discussed this before, I want to show the relationship to the verse above.

> *"…Come up hither, and I will show things*
> *<u>which must be hereafter</u>." (Revelation 4:1)*

Continued from above:

Thighs of bronze, its legs of iron, its feet partly of iron and partly of clay. The King watched while a stone was cut out without hands, which struck the image on its feet of iron and clay, and broke them in pieces. Then the iron, the clay, the bronze, the silver, and the gold were crushed together, the stone that crushed the image became a great mountain and filled the whole earth.

The head of gold represented the Babylon Empire that was in power at the time of the Kings dream. The Empire represented by the silver was the Mede/Persia Kingdom and was inferior to the Babylon Kingdom. The next world power represented by bronze was the Greek empire under Alexander the Great. Then comes the Iron Kingdom, this is the Roman Empire. The Romans were in power in Jesus day, and He predicted they would destroy Jerusalem and the Temple, and the people would be scattered to the four corners of the world. Jesus also said "I will build my church". Since those days we have been in the church age that is why America has not been mentioned along with these other world powers. All the above had dealings with Israel in a conquering roll.

Four of these have already passed across the world's stage of history. There is yet one more world power to deal with, and also the "Rock cut out without hands to explain.

This last world power was mentioned in Nebuchadnezzar dream as having feet of part iron and part clay. Iron and clay don't mix. So this Kingdom will be part strong and part weak. This is the revival of the Roman Empire according to many bible scholars, and in which I agree with completely. It is also led by the Antichrist.

Now here is what is to happen. (One) the rapture of the church, (Two) a seven year period of time led by the Antichrist, he will make a convent with Israel and in the mist of the week (three and one half years), he will enter the Temple, that has been rebuilt in troublesome times. He will then enter the Holy of Holies and proclaim that he is god. This is the abomination of desolation spoken by Daniel the prophet, and confirmed by Christ. (Three) At the end of the seven year tribulation Christ will return to this world and He (The Rock Cut Out Without Hands) will destroy and crush all Gentiles powers, and then set up a Kingdom that shall never be destroyed.

Notes and Reflections

Notes and Reflections

Notes and Reflections

Chapter V

Daniel 9

Most all prophecy relates to the Hebrew people, and their Messiah. While chapter 2 above related to the gentile world powers, it was still how they related to the Jewish people. While both chapters deal with almost the same time line, there is much more to be understood from this chapter. Daniel's prayer is recorded in 9:2-19.

> *In the first of his reign I, Daniel, observed in the books the number of the years which was revealed as the word of the Lord to Jeremiah the prophet for the completion of the desolations of Jerusalem, namely, seventy years. So I gave my attention to the Lord God to seek Him by prayer and supplication, with fasting, sackcloth, and ashes. And I prayed to the Lord my God and confessed and said," Alas, O Lord, the great and awesome God, who keeps His commandment.*
> *(Daniel 9:1-4) NASB*

He sought to understand the seventy years of prophecy by the word of the Lord through Jeremiah the prophet. While Daniel was praying, the, the angel Gabriel came to tell Daniel of the Seventy weeks of prophecy,

Seventy weeks have been decreed for your people and your holy city, to finish the transgression, to make to make an end of sin, to make atonement for iniquity, to bring in everlasting righteousness, to seal up vision and prophecy, and to anoint the most holy place. So you are to know and discern that from of a decree to restore and rebuild Jerusalem until Messiah the Prince there will be seven weeks and sixty two weeks; (Daniel 9:24-26) NASB

Daniel's prophecies take us to the crucifixion of our Lord Jesus Christ. Then there is a parenthesis that we call the church age. After this the Bible again places the emphasis on dealing with God's people. The Jewish people, back in their land, and bringing in the kingdom of God. The tribulation is also described. Jesus had said "I will build my church." The church age was empowered at Pentecost (Acts 2:1-4). 69 weeks of years was fulfilled, before the church age. There remains, one week or seven years yet to be fulfilled with the nation of Israel.

The vision of the 70 weeks (Daniel 9:1- 27). This chapter may be hard to understand, but it is very important to the overall bible prophecy and if it is to be understood in the present day these weeks are weeks of years, and therefore the 70 weeks represent 490 years. Note these weeks of years relate to the Hebrew people. 9:24 makes this very clear, 70 weeks are determined. "FOR YOUR PEOPLE" (Israel), Your Holy City, (Jerusalem). The 62 weeks in this passage takes us from Daniel to the crucifixion of our Lord. In verse 24 and 27 speaks of God's judgment in the end times. This chapter describes the time from the angel's appearing to Daniel, until the time of the Antichrist.

Listed below are things that are yet future;

1. "To finish the transgression"- backsliding by the Hebrew nation will never again be apostate (v 24).
2. "To make an end of sin"-as a nation they will never make a practice of sin (v.24).
3. "To make reconciliation for iniquity"- they will be reconciled to God by faith (v.24).
4. "To bring in everlasting righteousness"-this is God's righteous kingdom established at Christ second coming (v24).
5. "To seal up the vision and prophecy"- it will all have come to pass and there will be no more need for prophecy (v24).
6. "To anoint "the Most Holy place and the kingdom temple (v.24)

There is two here who are referred to as prince, and they are not to be confused. In verse 25, the bible is speaking clearly of the Lord Jesus. Then in verse 26 and following the prince spoken of there is the Antichrist... "And the people of the prince who is to come shall destroy the city and the sanctuary..." This destruction took place in AD 70 under the Roman General, Titus. "The prince then that is to come". Is believed to be a roman, and he as the Antichrist will rule over the revived Roman Empire (the feet of iron and clay the last of the king of Babylon's dream), that we read of in Daniel chapter two. Isaiah chapter sixty one complements this chapter of Daniel.

Notes and Reflections:

Notes and Reflections:

Notes and Reflections:

Chapter VI

Prophecy of the End Time Aliens are Coming

They have already came and been here for some time. If this was a News report the reporter might say, "This just in". What I am about to tell you may seem very strange to the non- believer in God. I heard today on NBC, (1/15/14) that there are some who believe that aliens are directing the affairs of men on earth today. A few days before this I also heard it for the first time, I'm not for sure which network it was on. I suppose they were just quoting some person or organization. If they were student of the Bible they would know these things have been going on for a long, long time. They would also know as the time for the rapture of the church draws near those wars, murders and all kinds of ungodly things will grow worse. Yes this world is filled with angels and demons, (aliens), to those who do not believe. Following is some scriptures you may want to read; Joel 3:9-14, Daniel chapter 11, Daniel 9:26-27. Revelation 11:7, 12:7-17, 13:4-7, 17:14.

All of these things that are happening in the Middle East, and around the world, if you think that this is just of men then my friend you are mistaken. More and more people are becoming demon possessed, and the kind of things they are capable of doing is to enter crowded theaters, or schools, and just start shooting seemly without reason, and setting off bombs in order to kill innocent people, then there is people doing things with cars that normal people would not be expected to do. Do not expect for it to get better, for it will get worse and worse as we approach the time of the rapture of the church. But it will be much worse in the tribulation. Hear what Paul has to say on this matter.

> *Let no man deceive you by ant means; for that day shall*
> *not come, except there come a falling away first, and that*
> *man of sin be reveled, the son of perdition; Who opposeth*
> *and exalteth himself above all that is called God or that*
> *is worshiped; so that he as God sitteth in the temple of*
> *God, shewing himself that he is God. Remember ye not,*
> *that, when I was with you, I told you these things? And*
> *now ye know what witholdeth that he might be revealed*
> *in his time. For the mystery of iniquity doth already work:*
> *only he who now lettethwill let until he is taken out of*
> *the way. (the Holy Spirit, at the rapture of the church)*
> *And then shall that wicked be revealed, whom the Lord*
> *shall consume with spirit of his mouth, and shall destroy*
> *with the brightness of His coming: Even him, whose*
> *coming is after the working of Satan with all power and*
> *signs and lying wonders, And with all deceivableness of*
> *unrighteousness in them that perish; because they received*
> *not the love of the truth, that they might be saved. And for*
> *this cause God shall send them strong delusion, that they*
> *should believe a lie; that they all might be damned who*
> *believe not the truth, but had pleasure in unrighteousness.*
> *(2 Thessalonians 2:3-12)*

When Daniel Interprets the King of Babylon's dream, one of the things he tells him, "the God of Heaven is revealing to the king what will be in the latter days". (Dan. 2:28). So far all that God has said up to this point has been true, and we can have confidence that all God say's that is yet to happen will come to pass. The balance of this chapter we will write concerning Daniel chapter twelve, it is a short chapter, Only 13 verses long but all about the end times, this chapter relates to the last seven years of gentile rule. The angel Michel, who is the special Prince over the Hebrew people, will stand up for these people, and a great war breaks out in heaven and on earth. Satan is thrown out of Heaven.

> *"And war broke out in heaven: Michel and his angels*
> *fought with the dragon; and the dragon and his angels*
> *fought, but they did not prevail, nor was a place found*
> *for them in heaven any longer. So the great dragon*
> *was cast out, that serpent of old, called the Devil and*
> *Satan, who deceived; the whole world was cast to*
> *the earth, and his angels were cast out with him."*
> *(Revelation 12:7-9 NKJ)*

Next; Daniel speaks of a time of trouble such as never was since there was a nation. Jesus also speaks of this time.

> *"When ye therefore shall see the abomination of*
> *desolation, spoken of by Daniel the prophet, stand in the*
> *holy place, (whoso readeth, let him understand :) Then let*
> *them which be in Judaea flee into the mountains: let him*
> *that is on the housetop not come down to take anything*
> *out of his house: Neither let him that is in the field return*
> *back to take his clothes, And woe unto them that are*
> *with child, and unto that give suck in those days! But*
> *pray ye that your flight is not in the winter, neither on the*
> *Sabbath day: For then there shall be great tribulation,*

such as was not since the beginning of the world to
this time, no nor ever shall be. (Matthew 24:15-21)

And finally Daniel the prophet says,

"And at that time" (<u>during this seven year period</u>)
your people shall be delivered;" (Daniel 12:1)

They will go through the tribulation with the rest of the world. In verse two speaks of the resurrection.

And many of them that sleep in the dust of the
earth shall awake, some to everlasting life and
some to shame and everlasting contempt.
(Daniel 12:2)

In the tribulation there will be 'One hundred and forty-four thousand of all the tribes of the children of Israel were sealed (these are Jewish evangelist,

And then a great mulitude … of all nations
standing before the throne and before the
Lamb… "Revelation 7:4-10".

Those spoken of in Revelation above are the same as those spoken of in Daniel 12: they are characterized as the wise

And they that be wise shall shine as the brightness
of the firmament; and they that turn many to
righteousness as the stars for ever and ever.
(Daniel 12:3)

*"But you Daniel, shut up the words, and seal the
book untill the time of the end;" (verse. 4a).*

During the Old Testament this was a sealed book. For one reason
the church age was a mystery to them, they looked for the conquering
Messiah and not the suffering Messiah. Another way to say this, is there
vision skipped over the church age to the very end of the tribulation
when Christ comes back and defeats all gentile rule, establishes Israel in
the land that God gave them and brings in the eternal kingdom of God.
Today as we have entered into the end times and see much of the end
times prophecies being fulfilled before our eyes this book is not so sealed
to us today. There is a great divide here between verse 4a, and verse 4b.

*"Many shall run to and fro, and
knowledge shall be increased."
(Verse 4b)*

Maybe when Columbus sailed to this land, there may have been
those trying to understand prophecy and thought is this what the Bible is
talking about. But today as we look at the air traffic map on TV, it looks
like a giant spider web, and this is multiplied across the world. There is
an interesting prophecy in the book of Nahum, it is found in chapter two.

*For the Lord has turned away the excellency of Jacob,
as the excellency of Israel; for the emptiers have emptied
them out, and marred their vine branches. The shield
of his mighty men is made red, the valiant men are in
scarlet; the chariots shall be with flaming torches in the
day of his preparation, and the fir trees shall be terribly
shaken. The chariots shall rage in the streets, they
shall justle one against another in the broad ways: they*

shall seem like torches, they shall run like the lightings.
He shall recount his worthies; they shall stumble in
their walk; they shall make haste to the wall thereof,
and the defense shall be prepared. (Nahum 2:2-5)

This scripture in verse 2, makes it clear that this is the time of the second coming of Christ, for the Lord will restore Israel, and it is clearly in this part of history of the world, one can look at our streets and Interstates at night and see the vehicles with their bright lights, and listen to the traffic reports to understand how the prophet Nahum would have expressed this in his day. However I believe he was referring to tanks and armored equipment of war without really knowing what it meant.

Notes and Reflections:

Notes and Reflections:

Notes and Reflections:

Chapter VII

The Alignment of Nations

There are two separate alignments of nations that we need to pay attention to. One is the European nations that are referred to in prophecy as the revived Roman Empire. The second is the nations that will be headed by Russia. This confederation of nations will move against Israel during the tribulation. These two groups are putting pressure on each other at this time, and this will speed up the preparation on both sides. This is a very explosive situation, and one more reason that I believe the rapture is about to take place.

I will start with the group that will have Russia as its head. You will find the account that I am about to report on in the book of Ezekiel, chapters thirty eight, and thirty nine. I highly encourage you to read these two chapters. When we study the people of Russia we find that they are descendants of Japheth who was a son of Noah. The names of the sons of Japheth were Gomer, Magog, Madal, Javan, Tubal, Mesheck, and Tiras. The sons of Gomer were Ashnkenaz, Riphath, and Togarmah. The sons of Javan were Elishah, Tarshish, Kittam, and Dodanim. From these the coastland peoples of the gentiles were separated into their lands, everyone according to language, according to their families into their nations.

Now these are the generations of the sons of Noah, Shem,
Ham, and Japheth; and unto them were sons born after
the flood. The sons of Japheth; Gomer, and Magog,
and Madai, and Javan, and Tubal, and Meshech,
and Tiras. And the sons of Gomer; Ashkenaz, and
Riphath, Togarmah. And the sons of Javan; Elishah,
and Tarshish, Kittim, and Dodanim. By these were
the isles of the Gentiles divided in their lands; every one
after his tongue, after their families, in their nations.
(Genesis 10:1-5)

The latter part of this would be countries that basely make up the European Union, England, France, Germany, etc. All descendents of Japheth. Gog is the ruler of Russia, Magog is Moscow, and Tubal according to some was the capitol of agriculture, at least another important city, Rosh (Russia). God is going to lead them out by putting hooks in their jaws. What are these hooks that God will use? Economical hard ship! Today as I write the USA and the European Union are placing sanction on Russia, and threaten more sanctions. The best proof I can show of this is to print a portion of this scripture.

THE HOOKS ARE CAST

And I will turn you about, and put hooks in your
jaws, and I will bring you forth, and all thine army,
horses and horseman, all of them clothed with all
sorts of armor, even a great company with bucklers
and shield, all of them handling swords. Persia, (Iran)
Ethiopia, and Put with them, all of them with shields
and helmet; Gomer and all his bands; the house of

> *Togarmah of the north quarters, and all his bands;*
> *and many people with thee. (Ezekiel 38: 4-6)*

The economy of Russia and Iran is under attack and it seems it could get much worse; this is the method that the USA and Europe have chosen to punish Russia for their part in bringing down the Air Liner with three hundred people, who all died, and for supporting the rebels against their homeland.

> *Sheba and Dedan and the merchants of Tarshish,*
> *with all the young lions thereof, shall say unto thee,*
> *Art thou come to take a spoil? Hast thou gathered thy*
> *company to take a prey? To carry away silver and gold,*
> *to take away cattle and goods, to take a great spoil?*
> *(Ezekiel 38: 13)*

The rest of chapter thirty-eight, and thirty -nine describes Gods judgment on Gog the ruler of this ungodly confederation. I believe this ruler is none other than Putin himself.

> *"For seven months the house of Israel will be burying*
> *them, in order to cleanse the land." (Ezekiel 39:12)*

The second group that we need to pay attention to is the revived Roman Empire who will be led by the Antichrist. The Bible teaches that people will not know who the Antichrist is until after the rapture, the rapture will happen in the twinkling of an eye. Though many will speck elate on who he is including me. And know I will not share my thoughts on this even if I were to be asked to. In Daniel chapter seven he has a vision of a beast with ten horns, this represents the ten nations of the revived Roman Empire, then he sees a little horn come up among them, this little horn represents the Antichrist. "The Antichrist will make a covenant with many for one week (seven years). But in the middle of the week He shall bring an end to sacrifice and offerings. And on the wings of abomination shall be one who makes desolate" (Daniel 10:27). Jesus quotes from this scripture in Daniel, and warns His people that when they see the abomination spoken of by Daniel the prophet...

> *"Let those who are in Judea flee to the mountains"*
> *(Matthew 24:15-24).*

Israel will come under great tribulation at that time. In Matthew chapter's twenty-four and twenty-five, are the words of Jesus describing His second coming, the rapture had taken place at least seven years before this, and now Jesus the Christ is taken care of some house cleaning chores, before bringing in His EVERLASSTING KINGDOM! The last verse of this discourse states

> *"And these will go away into everlasting*
> *punishment, but the righteous into eternal life"*
> *(Matthew 25; 46).*

The righteous here are those who were saved in the tribulation period, all of those saved before the tribulation are already with Jesus, at the time Jesus was speaking of here.

There will be upheavals in nature Jesus said;

> *"For nation will rise against nation, and kingdom*
> *against kingdom, and there will* ***be earthquakes***
> *in divers places, and there shall be famines and*
> *troubles. These are the beginning of sorrows."*
> *(Mark 13:8)*

In this 13th chapter Jesus speaks of the signs of the time and the end of the age. In the news today they are speaking of all the earthquakes that are happening in California, and predicting a much larger earthquake that they believe will happen in southern California. In Revelation many of these upheavals in nature are mentioned, we need to remember that what happens before the tribulation are just warnings of much greater events to happen during this seven year period that is called the tribulation. These events are God's mercy to all unbelievers calling them to repentance. Our Lord does not wish for you to go through this terrible time that we have been writing on.

> *"The Lord is not slack concerning His promises,*
> *as some men count slackness; but is long suffering*
> *to us-ward, not willing that any should perish,*
> *but that all should come to repentance"*
> *(2-Peter 3:9).*

> *"Then the angel took the censer, filled it with fire of the*
> *alter, and cast it into the earth. And there were voices,*
> *and thundering, and lighting, and an earthquake"*
> *(Revelation 8:5).*

In Revelation chapter nineteen Christ descends from heaven, and along with chapter twenty, shows how the satanic rebellion is crushed. The reason I refer to this section of Revelation is so I can call the reader's attention to the flesh eating birds of the air.

> *"And I saw an angel standing in the sun; and he cried with*
> *a loud voice, saying to all the fowls that fly in the mist of*
> *heaven, Come and gather together unto the supper of the*
> *great God. That ye may eat the flesh of kings, and the flesh of*

*captains, and the flesh of mighty men, and the flesh of horses
and of them who sit on them, and the flesh of all men, both
free and slave, both small and great." (Revelation 19:17-18)*

Snow owls who normally live in the artic has been spotted recently in Virginia, and as far south as Florida, and at Boston Logan Airport, One that was captured for a while, when released flew south instead of north. I have also been told that the buzzard population is on the increase. Other scripture that mention these flesh eating birds is, Leviticus 11:13-20, Deuteronomy 14:12-19. Finally you can read of Gods judgments on the nations and these birds are mentioned in Isaiah chapter thirty- four. (It is possible the white owl mentioned in the scripture and the snow owl of the artic are the same, if so God's Spirit has already started calling them home. ARE WE THERE YET? Soon children, soon!

In the near future all over this world the cry will go out GONE!, GONE! Maybe today!

Summary

The author of this book is an 87 year old retired Minister, with many years of studying the word of God, and I believe with all my heart that I will be one of those taken while still alive at the rapture of the church. I also believe that very soon the church will be <u>GONE!!</u>

INTRODUCTION:

Explains the title of the book. Also Jesus we cannot know the day or the hour of His coming, <u>But we are to know the season!</u>

CHAPTER ONE:

Gives a description of the rapture of the church.

CHAPTURE TWO:

Deals with some of the terrible signs of these last days.

CHAPTER THREE:

Things that are yet to happen.

CHAPTER FOUR:

Shows the capture of Israel by the Babylon's, and takes us through the following world powers that control Israel, up until the church age. It then skips over the church age, and resumes its prophecy with the Roman revived Empire.

CHAPTER FIVE:

Deals with almost the same time line as chapter four, yet there is much more to be understood from this chapter.

CHAPTER SIX:

Describes the last seven years of Gentile rule.

CHAPTER SEVEN:

The alignment of nations, speaks of the confederate of nations that will be led by Russia, in the last days. And also about the revived Roman Empire Led by the Antichrist.